PEARLS

WISDOM & GRACE

PEARLS

Mary Drum (B.Th)

GRACE

INTRODUCTION

Grace is god's own loving kindness and favour toward human beings, given freely so we can respond to his call to become children of God. Grace is participation in the life of God.

PEARLS: WISDOM & GRACE

The Bible is God's word written by human hands under the wise, guiding influence of God's Spirit. And the wisdom texts in the Bible especially show divine discernment at work.

Even more so, we see wisdom at work in the ministry of Jesus Christ. The wisdom he exercises is, again, like the Scriptures, at one with the wisdom of the Holy Spirit.

True human wisdom – so the Scriptures affirm – is a gift from God, and it points out the folly of trusting in worldly human wisdom to discern what is required of us to live a good life. This book of PEARLS comprises moments of wisdom from the word of God that will show us how to live a good life.

It is a curious thing to be writing these words. For many years I have looked at the collection of photographs that illustrate the GRACE books. They have always spoken to me of the greatness of God-created humanity. While others might merely see people being people, my faith allows me to see revealed in the images both God's design and the human heart's response to its creator and to other human beings created by God. God initiates a covenant of loving kindness with us to which we can choose to respond in love.

There has never been a time in my life when I did not have faith in God or his providence; and PEARLS, SALT and HEART are part of my response to God's providential care.

PEARLS is a considered collection of wisdom excerpts from the Sacred Scriptures. When we recognise that wisdom ultimately comes from God, and that it is given to us to live a good life, we can see how to be happy, not only in relation to ourselves, but in relation to our families, friends and indeed the rest of God's creation. A good life though is not an easy life: it is a life of goodness which we can build through all that we experience.

ECCLESIASTES 3:1-13

There is a time for everything, and a season for every activity under heaven: a time to be born and a time to die, a time to plant and a time to uproot, a time to kill and a time to heal, a time to tear down and a time to build, a time to weep and a time to laugh, a time to mourn and a time to dance, a time to scatter stones and a time to gather them, a time to embrace and a time to refrain, a time to search and a time to give up, a time to keep and a time to throw away, a time to tear and a time to mend, a time to be silent and a time to speak, a time to love and a time to hate, a time for war and a time for peace. What does the worker gain from his toil? I have seen the burden God has laid on men. He has made everything beautiful in its time.

He has also set eternity in the hearts of men; yet they cannot fathom what God has done from beginning to end. I know that there is nothing better for men than to be happy and do good while they live. That everyone may eat and drink, and find satisfaction in all his toil – this is the gift of God.

WISDOM

ISAIAH 28:29 All this also comes from the LORD Almighty, wonderful in counsel and magnificent in wisdom.

PROVERBS 19:8 He who gets wisdom loves his own soul; he who cherishes understanding prospers.

ECC 10:12

Words from a wise man's mouth
are gracious.

PROVERBS 2:1-5
My son, if you accept my
words and store up my
commands within you,

turning your ear to wisdom
and applying your heart to
understanding,

and if you call out for insight
and cry aloud for
understanding,

and if you look for it as for
silver and search for it as for
hidden treasure,

then you will understand the
fear of the LORD and find the
knowledge of God.

ECCLESIASTES 12:6-7

Remember him – before the
silver cord is severed, or the
golden bowl is broken; before
the pitcher is shattered at the
spring, or the wheel broken at
the well, and the dust returns
to the ground it came from,
and the spirit returns to God
who gave it.

PROVERBS 2:6-11
For the LORD gives wisdom,
and from his mouth come
knowledge and
understanding.

He holds victory in store for the
upright, he is a shield to those
whose walk is blameless,

for he guards the course of
the just and protects the way
of his faithful ones.

Then you will understand
what is right and just and
fair – every good path.

For wisdom will enter your
heart, and knowledge will
be pleasant to your soul.

Discretion will protect you, and
understanding will guard you.

PROVERBS 4:5-9

Get wisdom, get understanding; do not forget my words or swerve from them. Do not forsake wisdom, and she will protect you; love her, and she will watch over you. Wisdom is supreme; therefore get wisdom.

Though it cost all you have, get understanding. Esteem her, and she will exalt you; embrace her, and she will honour you. She will set a garland of grace on your head and present you with a crown of splendour.

PR 4:10-15

Listen, my son, accept what I say, and the years of your life will be many. I guide you in the way of wisdom and lead you along straight paths.

When you walk, your steps will not be hampered; when you run, you will not stumble. Hold on to instruction, do not let it go; guard it well, for it is your life.

Do not set foot on the path of the wicked or walk in the way of evil men. Avoid it, do not travel on it; turn from it and go on your way.

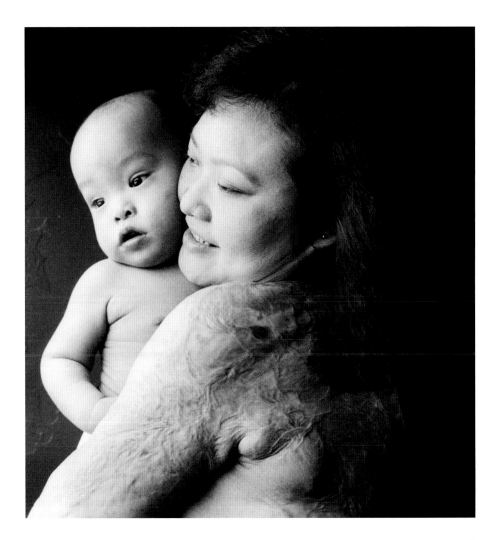

PROVERBS 4:20-26

My son, pay attention to what
I say; listen closely to my
words.

Do not let them out of your
sight, keep them within your
heart;

for they are life to those who
find them and health to
a man's whole body.

Above all else, guard your
heart, for it is the wellspring
of life.

Put away perversity from your
mouth; keep corrupt talk far
from your lips.

Let your eyes look straight
ahead, fix your gaze directly
before you.

Make level paths for your feet
and take only ways that are
firm.

ECCLESIASTES 5:3
As a dream comes when
there are many cares, so the
speech of a fool when there
are many words.

ECC 5:3

JOY & HAPPINESS

PSALM 143:10 Let your spirit lead me on a level path.

True joy and happiness derive from sound, mature knowledge of God and from finding joy in his works and faithfulness. As knowledge of God and faith call us to live a good life, our guide for the journey is God's Spirit.

Paul reminds us in his letter to the Galatians that the fruits of the Spirit are perfections that may be formed divinely within us when we cooperate with God's Spirit. They include: charity, joy, peace, patience, kindness, goodness, generosity, gentleness, faithfulness, modesty, self-control, and chastity (cf. Galatians 5:22).

Life is often difficult. Ultimately, true happiness and joy are to be found in eternal life in God, not in the riches of our own making apart from God.

Ecclesiastes 3:12-13
I know that there is nothing
better for men than to be
happy and do good while
they live. That everyone may
eat and drink, and find
satisfaction in all his toil –
this is the gift of God.

ROMANS 8:14-15
Because those who are led
by the Spirit of God are sons
of God.

For you did not receive a spirit
that makes you a slave again
to fear, but you received the
Spirit of sonship. And by him
we cry, "Abba, Father."

Ro 8:14-15

LUKE 6:17-23

He went down with them and stood on a level place. A large crowd of his disciples was there and a great number of people from all over Judea, from Jerusalem, and from the coast of Tyre and Sidon, who had come to hear him and to be healed of their diseases. Those troubled by evil spirits were cured, and the people all tried to touch him, because power was coming from him and healing them all. Looking at his disciples, he said:

"Blessed are you who are poor, for yours is the kingdom of God. Blessed are you who hunger now, for you will be satisfied. Blessed are you who weep now, for you will laugh. Blessed are you when men hate you, when they exclude you and insult you and reject your name as evil, because of the Son of Man.

"Rejoice in that day and leap for joy, because great is your reward in heaven. For that is how their fathers treated the prophets."

Lk 6:17-23

LUKE 6:37-42

"Do not judge, and you will not be judged. Do not condemn, and you will not be condemned. Forgive, and you will be forgiven. Give, and it will be given to you. A good measure, pressed down, shaken together and running over, will be poured into your lap. For with the measure you use, it will be measured to you." He also told them this parable: "Can a blind man lead a blind man? Will they not both fall into a pit? A student is not above his teacher, but everyone who is fully trained will be like his teacher.

"Why do you look at the speck of sawdust in your brother's eye and pay no attention to the plank in your own eye? How can you say to your brother, 'Brother, let me take the speck out of your eye,' when you yourself fail to see the plank in your own eye? You hypocrite, first take the plank out of your eye, and then you will see clearly to remove the speck from your brother's eye."

Luke 6:43-45
No good tree bears bad fruit,
nor does a bad tree bear
good fruit.

Each tree is recognised by its
own fruit. People do not pick
figs from thornbushes, or
grapes from briers.

The good man brings good
things out of the good stored
up in his heart, and the evil
man brings evil things out of
the evil stored up in his heart.
For out of the overflow of his
heart his mouth speaks.

41

Ecc 5:18-19

ECCLESIASTES 5:18-19
Then I realised that it is good
and proper for a man to eat
and drink, and to find
satisfaction in his toilsome
labour under the sun during
the few days of life God has
given him – for this is his lot.
Moreover, when God gives
any man wealth and
possessions, and enables him
to enjoy them, to accept his
lot and be happy in his work –
this is a gift of God.

ECCLESIASTES 5:20
He seldom reflects on the days
of his life, because God keeps
him occupied with gladness of
heart.

Go, eat your food with
gladness, and drink your wine
with a joyful heart, for it is now
that God favours what you do.

ECCLESIASTES 7:14

When times are good, be happy; but when times are bad, consider: God has made the one as well as the other.

PROVERBS 10:9

The man of integrity walks securely.

PROVERBS 12:20
There is deceit in the hearts of
those who plot evil, but joy for
those who promote peace

PROVERBS 24:13-14
Eat honey, my son, for it is
good; honey from the comb
is sweet to your taste.

Know also that wisdom is
sweet to your soul; if you find
it, there is a future hope for
you, and your hope will not
be cut off.

REVELATION 7:17
For the Lamb at the center
of the throne will be their
shepherd; he will lead them
to springs of living water. And
God will wipe away every
tear from their eyes.

FAMILY

MATTHEW 19:19 Honour your father and mother, and love your neigbour as yourself.

The Western view of the nuclear family narrows the scope of the term, 'family'. The people of the ancient Near East, including the tribes of Israel, had a broader, more extended understanding of the term which is often reflected in the Bible. This can be seen especially in, for example, the life of Jesus.

Families ideally protect, comfort and nurture human persons, and the Holy Family displays these roles. The human person, Jesus, is among the fruits of this particular holy family; he is the human person *par excellence*. Jesus teaches us that God has always considered all his children of faith, the people of God, to be his family.

GENESIS 1:26-28

Then God said, "Let us make man in our image, in our likeness, and let them rule over the fish of the sea and the birds of the air, over the livestock, over all the earth, and over all the creatures that move along the ground." So God created man in his own image, in the image of God he created him; male and female he created them. God blessed them and said to them, "Be fruitful and increase in number; fill the earth and subdue it. Rule over the fish of the sea and the birds of the air and over every living creature that moves on the ground."

GALATIANS 6:10
Therefore, as we have
opportunity, let us do good
to all people, especially to
those who belong to the
family of believers.

A man who loves wisdom
brings joy to his father.

PROVERBS 29:3

PSALM 68:6
God sets the lonely in families.

MATTHEW 7:7-11

"Ask and it will be given to you; seek and you will find; knock and the door will be opened to you. For everyone who asks receives; he who seeks finds; and to him who knocks, the door will be opened.

"Which of you, if his son asks for bread, will give him a stone? Or if he asks for a fish, will give him a snake?

"If you, then, though you are evil, know how to give good gifts to your children, how much more will your Father in heaven give good gifts to those who ask him!"

MATTHEW 19:14
Jesus said, "Let the little
children come to me, and
do not hinder them, for the
kingdom of heaven belongs
to such as these."

1 TIMOTHY 5:7-8
Give the people these
instructions, too, so that no
one may be open to blame

If anyone does not provide for
his relatives, and especially for
his immediate family, he has
denied the faith and is worse
than an unbeliever.

JOHN 1:12

Yet to all who received him, to those who believed in his name, he gave the right to become children of God.

PSALM 103:13
As a father has compassion
on his children, so the LORD
has compassion on those who
fear him.

PROVERBS 17:6

PROVERBS 17:6
Children's children are a
crown to the aged, and
parents are the pride of
their children.

PROVERBS 18:22
He who finds a wife finds what
is good and receives favour
from the LORD.

PROVERBS 10:1

A wise son brings joy to his father.

PROVERBS 19:14
Houses and wealth are
inherited from parents, but a
prudent wife is from the LORD.

PROVERBS 23:15
My son, if your heart is wise,
then my heart will be glad

FRIENDSHIP

Proverbs 3:3-4 Let love and faithfulness never leave you; bind them around your neck, write them on the tablet of your heart. Then you will win favour and a good name in the sight of God and man.

God designed us as relational human persons, not as mere isolated human beings. Even religious who spend their lives in contemplation and prayer are connected to the world for which they pray. We need friends; they are a gift from God. We need to respect them accordingly.

ECCLESIASTES 4:9-12

Two are better than one, because they have a good return for their work.

If one falls down, his friend can help him up. But pity the man who falls and has no one to help him up!

Also, if two lie down together, they will keep warm. But how can one keep warm alone?

Though one may be over-powered, two can defend themselves. A cord of three strands is not quickly broken.

1 Samuel 20:42

Jonathan said to David, "Go in peace, for we have sworn friendship with each other in the name of the LORD, saying, 'The LORD is witness between you and me, and between your descendants and my descendants forever.'" Then David left, and Jonathan went back to the town.

PROVERBS 12:16
A fool shows his annoyance
at once, but a prudent man
overlooks an insult.

PROVERBS 12:25
An anxious heart weighs a
man down, but a kind word
cheers him up.

PROVERBS 17:9
He who covers over an
offence promotes love, but
whoever repeats the matter
separates close friends.

EPHESIANS 4:1-2 As a prisoner for the LORD, then, I urge you to live a life worthy of the calling you have received. Be completely humble and gentle; be patient, bearing with one another in love.

PROVERBS 18:24
A man of many companions
may come to ruin, but there is
a friend who sticks closer than
a brother.

PROVERBS 27:10
Do not forsake your friend
and the friend of your father,
and do not go to your
brother's house when disaster
strikes you – better a neigbour
nearby than a brother
far away.

MATTHEW 27:55-56
Many women were there, watching from a distance. They had followed Jesus from Galilee to care for his needs. Among them were Mary Magdalene, Mary the mother of James and Joses, and the mother of Zebedee's sons.

JOB 42:10

After Job had prayed for his friends, the LORD made him prosperous again and gave him twice as much as he had before.

ROMANS 1:11-12
I long to see you so that I may
impart to you some spiritual
gift to make you strong –

that is, that you and I may be
mutually encouraged by each
other's faith

MATTHEW 7:12

So in everything, do to others
what you would have them
do to you, for this sums up the
Law and the Prophets.

TRUE WEALTH

Material possessions and wealth are gifts that originate from God. Used wisely, they can be a blessing for others, as well as for ourselves. For true wealth is found in wisdom and in living a good life.

PROVERBS 3:13-15

Blessed is the man who finds wisdom, the man who gains understanding

for she is more profitable than silver and yields better returns than gold.

She is more precious than rubies; nothing you desire can compare with her.

1SAMUEL 2:7-8

The LORD sends poverty and wealth; he humbles and he exalts.

He raises the poor from the dust and lifts the needy from the ash heap; he seats them with princes and has them inherit a throne of honour. For the foundations of the earth are the LORD'S; upon them he has set the world.

ECC 5:10-11

ECCLESIASTES 5:10-11
Whoever loves money never
has money enough; whoever
loves wealth is never satisfied
with his income. This too is
meaningless.

As goods increase, so do
those who consume them.

COLOSSIANS 2:2-3
My purpose is that they may
be encouraged in heart and
united in love, so that they
may have the full riches of
complete understanding, in
order that they may know the
mystery of God, namely, Christ,
in whom are hidden all the
treasures of wisdom and
knowledge.

EPHESIANS 1:7
In him we have redemption
through his blood, the
forgiveness of sins, in
accordance with the riches
of God's grace

2 CORINTHIANS 9:10-11
Now he who supplies seed to the sower and bread for food will also supply and increase your store of seed and will enlarge the harvest of your righteousness.

2 COR 9:10-11

You will be made rich in every way so that you can be generous on every occasion, and through us your generosity will result in thanksgiving to God.

ROMANS 11:33

Oh, the depth of the riches of the wisdom and knowledge of God! How unsearchable his judgments, and his paths beyond tracing out!

HEBREWS 13:5-6
Keep your lives free from the love of money and be content with what you have, because God has said, "Never will I leave you; never will I forsake you."

So we say with confidence, "The Lord is my helper; I will not be afraid. What can man do to me?"

1 Timothy 6:6-8
But godliness with
contentment is great gain.

For we brought nothing into
the world, and we can take
nothing out of it.

But if we have food and
clothing, we will be content
with that.

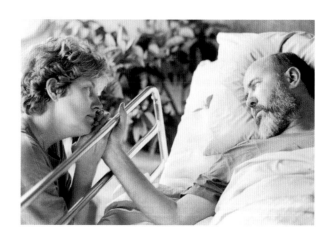

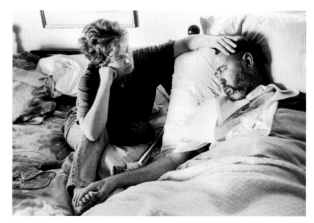

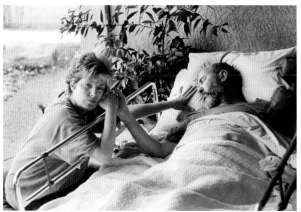

PROVERBS 21:1-3
The king's heart is in the hand
of the LORD; he directs it like
a watercourse wherever he
pleases.

All a man's ways seem right to
him, but the LORD weighs the
heart.

To do what is right and just is
more acceptable to the LORD
than sacrifice.

PROVERBS 13:8

A man's riches may ransom his life,
but a poor man hears no threat.

1 J~N~ 3:17

I JOHN 3:17
If anyone has material
possessions and sees his
brother in need but has no
pity on him, how can the love
of God be in him?

I keep asking that the God of our Lord Jesus Christ, the glorious Father, may give you the Spirit of wisdom and revelation, so that you may know him better. I pray also that the eyes of your heart may be enlightened in order that you may know the hope to which he has called you, the riches of his glorious inheritance in the saints.

PROVERBS 8:19-21
My fruit is better than fine
gold; what I yield surpasses
choice silver. I walk in the way
of righteousness, along the
paths of justice, bestowing
wealth on those who love me,
and making their treasures full.

LUKE 12:23 Life is more than food, and the body more than clothes.

Acknowledgements

All images in *Pearls* were originally published by **M ▪ I ▪ L ▪ K**™ Publishing Limited and have been used under licence from **M ▪ I ▪ L ▪ K**™ Licensing Limited, all rights reserved. www.milkphotos.com

The images are Copyright © the individual photographers as follows.

p8 and cover Andrei Jewell
p15 Thanh Long
p16 and cover Louise Gubb
p18 and cover Duane Prentice
p21 Stephen Hathaway
p23 and cover Anne Bayin
p24 and cover John Kaplan
p28 Pat Justis
pp30-31 John Kaplan
pp32-33 Jinjun Mao
p34 José Martí
p37 Heather Pillar
pp38-39 Sombut Ketkeaw
p40-41 Kailas Soni
p43 John Siu
p44 Vladimir Kryukov
p46 J D Nielsen
p49 Greg Williams
p51 Rajib De
pp52-53 Damrong Juntawonsup
pp54-55 and cover
P Kevin Morley

p56 Aranya Sen
p60 Sam Tanner
p63 Deborah Roundtree
p65 Aris Pavlos
pp66-67 King Tuang Wong
p68 and cover Gerald Botha
p71 Michael Chiabaudo
p73 Luca Trovato
p74 and cover John A Hryniuk
p76 Mark Engledow
p78 Deborah Roundtree
p79 Stephen McAlpine
pp80-81 Manfred Witz
p82 Terry Winn
p85 and cover
Everett Kennedy Brown
p86 John McNamara
p91 Philip Hight
pp92-93 Dharmesh Bhavsar
p94-95 Serena Stevenson
p97 Cristina Piza
p98 Rashid Un Nabi

p101 Mara Catalán
p103 Paul Carter
p104 Linda Pottage
p107 and cover Mike Ryan
pp108-109 Tamas Kovacs
p110 and cover Linda Heim
pp114-115 Quoc Tuan
p116 Jim Witmer
p119 Josef Sekal
pp120-121 and cover Yew Fatt Siew
p122 Madan Mahatta
p125 Kostas Argyris
pp128-129 William Foley
p130 Tomas D W Friedmann
pp132-133 Jack Dykinga
pp134-135 David Tak-Wai Leung
p136 Debashis Mukherjee (Deba)
p139 Gary Freeman
p140 Les Slesnick
p143 Wilfred van Zyl
p145 and cover Milo Stewart Jr.

Published by St Pauls Publications, PO Box 906, Strathfield NSW 2135 Australia,
www.stpauls.com.au

This edition published in 2007 by St Pauls Publications in association with Drum Publishing Pty
Ltd under license from M.I.L.K. Licensing Ltd. Title and concept Copyright © 2007 Mary
Drum Pty Ltd. The right of Mary Drum to be identified as author of this work has been asserted
by her in accordance with the Copyright, Designs and Patents Act 1988.

British Library Cataloguing Data.
A catalogue record for this book is available from the British Library.

Designed by Carolyn Lewis.
Printed and bound by 1010 Printing International Ltd, China.